Introduction to
WATERCOLOURS

igloobooks

Published in 2015
by Igloo Books Ltd
Cottage Farm
Sywell
NN6 0BJ
www.igloobooks.com

Cover images © Thinkstock / Getty Images

LEO002 0715
2 4 6 8 10 9 7 5 3 1
ISBN 978-1-78440-282-2

Printed and manufactured in China

Introduction to

WATERCOLOURS

Contents

Getting to know watercolours 6
Artists' tools 8
Other materials 14
Choosing a subject 16
Ready to paint 18
Colour wheel 20
Mixing colours 22
Wet into wet 24
Wet on dry 26
Combining wet and dry 30
Dry brush 32
Blending 34
Brushwork 36
Choosing a subject 38
Landscapes 40
Portraits 42
Animals 44
Still life 46

Getting to know watercolours

Artists' tools

There are several tools that you will need to paint with watercolours. Brushes, paper, and of course your paints. You'll also need extra equipment, such as a palette and storage for your finished artwork.

Brushes

Watercolour brushes are softer than those used for oil and acrylic painting. There are many different kinds of brush for you to choose from. They vary in size and shape and their bristles may be made from either natural or synthetic fibres. Brushes made from natural fibres, such as sable, are typically much more expensive than their synthetic counterparts. Sometimes, manufacturers will mix sable bristles with cheaper hair, such as squirrel or camel hair, to reduce the cost. If you are choosing synthetic brushes, you will need those with softer bristles.

Brush size

Brushes are usually numbered – for example, a range of brushes may start with No0000, which is suitable for only fine work, and end with No20, which is very large. Each manufacturer's number system may be slightly different, so No3 in one range may not be the same size as No3 in a different range. Flat brushes may be numbered by the total bristle width.

Brush shape

Brushes vary in shape, depending on the type of mark you want to make. The most commonly used shapes include round, flat or chisel headed, filbert and fan. Round brushes have a rounded ferrule (the metal sleeve that joins the bristles to the brush handle). Large round brushes are used for laying a wash and a wide expanse of colour. Flat or chisel headed brushes have a flattened ferrule with a square-cut bristle head. The wide bristles are good for applying paint in short dabs, while the narrow bridges are better for finer details. Filbert brushes are somewhere in between round and flat brushes. They have a flattened ferrule with tapered bristles and are especially versatile. Fan brushes have splayed out bristles and are used for blending colours.

Brush care

Rinse your brushes well each time you use them but never leave them standing in water. At the end of a painting session, wash your brushes well in warm, soapy water then rinse them in clean water. Reshape the bristles and store them upright with the handle-end down.

Paper

Choosing the right type of paper for your artwork is just as important as choosing your paints, because the type of paper you work on can greatly influence how your painting looks. The texture, weight and colour of paper should be carefully considered before you start to paint.

Texture

The texture of paper affects how paint is absorbed. Rough paper is heavily textured and is suitable for bold brushwork, but is not the best choice for beginners because it makes the washes very unpredictable. At the other end of the scale, hot-pressed (HP) paper has a very smooth surface and is often labelled as such. Due to the smoothness of this type of paper, the colour often stays on its surface and so can be manipulated more easily. HP paper is best for combining watercolour and pen-and-ink, and watercolour and coloured pencil. Somewhere between these two types of paper is cold-pressed, or NOT paper. This paper has a noticeable texture and is the best choice for most watercolours.

Weight

The weight of paper determines its thickness and absorbency.
Paper weight is given in grams per square metre (gsm) or pounds (lb).
Lightweight paper is about 190 gsm (90 lb), medium paper weighs
around 300 gsm (140 lb) and heavy paper is around 638 gsm (300 lb).
Any paper that is 200 gsm (110 lb) or lighter will absorb paint and
so tends to buckle quite easily. This makes the paper unsuitable for
beginners. The most commonly used paper is 300 gsm (140 lb).

Colour

In addition to the texture and
weight of your paper, the colour is
also important. Many artists favour
a bright white paper. White paper
reflects light back through the paint,
which gives it translucence. It also
serves as the whitest and brightest
part of the painting. For works of art
that contain a lot of white using white
paper is advantageous because the
paper can simply be left unpainted.

Buying paper

A pad of watercolour paper is generally the most convenient
to buy. Usually the cover of the pad shows the characteristics
of the paper. If you are not sure what kind of paper you want
to paint on, most art supply shops will sell individual sheets
of paper. Unfortunately, individual sheets may have fingerprints
on them, left behind when people have examined the paper.
Fingers have natural oils that will mark paper. If you intend to
buy just a single sheet of paper, try to select one from the bottom
of the pile. Although most modern paper is now acid-free, it still
pays to check that paper is acid free before you purchase it.
Acid will slowly destroy your art.

Paints

Watercolour paints are made from mixing a finely ground pigment with a water-soluble gum binder or gum arabic solution. In the past, honey or sugar was added to the paint to make it more soluble, but today, glycerine is used instead. Today, paints come in pans or tubes with each having pros and cons.

Pans of paint

Pans are small, square cakes of pigment. They are either sold individually or in a paint box as a collection of different colours. Pans tend to be cheaper than tubes but can easily dry out, so in the long run it may be worth investing in tubes. To pick up the colour from a pan, you need to dampen your brush and move it over the colour.

Tubes

Generally, tubes are recommended once you know how to use and mix the colours in your paint box. Each tube contains a different colour. To use the colour, a small amount of paint is squeezed onto a clean, dry palette. Being able to squeeze the paint out of the tube means that it's easier to keep these paints clean but you may squeeze out too much colour and end up wasting paint. If this does happen, you can simply wet the paint on your palette and carry on using it. Tube paint can be cumbersome to work with because you have to stop painting to access the tube and mix the paint. However, it is easier to mix than pans and so is more suitable to painting larger areas.

Sunshine Yellow

Water Colours

Permanence A
Series 3

Sunshine Yellow • Sunshine Yellow
Sunshine Yellow • Sunshine Yellow

Manufacturer's name for colour

Printed colour

Lightfastness rating

Price group

Pigment name (in multiple languages)

Buying paints

There are several different brands to choose from. Whether you are buying larger tubes or small pans, it is better to have a few, better quality paints than more cheap paints. School paints are usually the cheapest watercolour paints but not the best quality. This is because they have a filler added to the pigment, which means that the colours they produce are not great.

Other materials

Once you have bought your paper, brushes and paints, and have access to water, you will need little more equipment to start painting. However, palettes, brush holders, brush boxes, easels and storage folders all make the process of painting much easier. In addition to these, you'll also need pencils and sketchpads to plan your work.

Palettes and palette boxes

While paint boxes usually have lids that are marked with palette divisions, if you are using tubes you will need a palette on which to mix your paint. Because mixing paint is such a vital step in the watercolour process, you need a palette to make this process as easy as possible. Palettes with mixing wells are the best type of palette to use because they allow you to keep your colours separate. To see the colours, a white palette is useful. Although you can buy plastic palettes, those made from porcelain are easier to clean and are preferred by many artists.

Brush holders

There are several types of paintbrush holder in which to keep your brushes while painting. They can be manufactured from a range of materials, from plastic and wood to Perspex. Whichever you choose, your brushes should stand upright and the bristles should not touch the bottom of the holder. Some holders have lids that seal so you can carry water in them, too. These are especially useful when painting outdoors. In addition to these holders, you can also buy brush storage boxes that are great for carrying and preserving your brushes. They come in a range of sizes so you need to consider how many brushes you have and their sizes before you buy one. If your box is too big for the quantity of brushes you have, the brushes may roll around in the box and become damaged.

Easels

Like any method of painting, watercolour work requires a firm surface on which to attach your paper. You can attach paper to a hard piece of wood with tape, clips and tacks so that your paper doesn't shift around or crinkle when you start painting. If you want to paint regularly, an easel is a good investment. Small tabletop easels are great for indoor use but are not very practical when painting outdoors. For outdoor use, a metal or box easel is preferable. Both have adjustable legs and can be set up on any flat surface. Box easels are especially useful because you can use them to store your paints and brushes while painting outdoors.

Storage folders

Art folders come in various shapes and sizes and are made from different materials. The simplest are made from cardboard, while more sophisticated folders are made from hard plastic. Some folders also come with plastic sheaves in which to put your art. These are great for viewing your work, too.

Choosing a subject

Finding inspiration

Often, being unable to find a subject is the hardest part of beginning a painting. Like authors who experience writer's block, many artists struggle to find the inspiration to get started. Once you feel inspired, finding a subject to paint should be easier.

Tidy workspace

Although it is a matter of personal taste, for many people trying to concentrate or indeed feel relaxed and creative is difficult when surrounded by mess. If you're lucky enough to have an area dedicated specifically for your painting, it may help if it is kept tidy and if your materials are kept in an orderly way. If you have not organised your paper and brushes, beginning to paint can be extremely difficult. If you paint in a space that is used for other things, such as at a dining-room table, try to remove anything that is not related to your painting. This will help to focus your mind on painting alone.

Arty jobs

If your workspace is tidy, you can get everything ready to start. Organise your paints in an order that works for you. Make sure that they are all clean and ready for you to start painting.

Clear your mind

Nothing clears your mind like exercise – you don't have to start a training regime, however! Instead, try a walk or a run. While you're exercising, you will take in fresh air and circulate oxygen around your body which will make you feel invigorated. As you walk or run, look around you to see the beauty everywhere. You may even stumble across something to paint.

Visit a gallery

Another great way to feel inspired is to take your inspiration from others. The best way to do this is to go to a gallery and surround yourself with art. If you don't have a nearby gallery, spend some time looking at art online, or in a book. Many artists have their own websites where you can see their art and also find out more about the work and artist.

Ready to paint

Now you're ready to paint, but what will you paint?
Andy Warhol painted movie stars, Degas painted
ballerinas and Monet was famous for his water lilies.
Throughout history, many artists have favoured one
particular subject and have become known for it.
So, how did they decide what to paint?

Paint your current life

It has always been said that writers should write about what they know. In many ways, the same can be said of artists. This is because if you paint what you know about, familiarity will fuel your confidence. If you are confident before you start to paint, you will feel bolder with your brush and more inclined to try something new. Knowing your subject will give you an innate knowledge of the finer details that are invaluable to painting precisely and accurately. However, continually painting familiar objects, people or scenes may lead to boredom, and sometimes you will need a change of subject.

Paint what interests you

For many people, one particular thing fascinates them. If you're interested in something, paint it! Even if it is something that you don't know very well, as long as you find it interesting you will enjoy painting it. You will still need to study it carefully before you start to paint it.

Paint what is around you

Many people are surrounded by subjects worthy of painting, without even realising it. Subjects such as your pets, a bowl of fruit on your kitchen counter or a musical instrument make for interesting things to paint. Try to find subjects that are rich or varied in colour, subjects that capture the light in an interesting way or subjects that have unusual angles. If you have a garden, there are undoubtedly many things within it that you could paint, from flowers in bloom to birds and insects that live there.

Know your limits

While there may be many things that inspire you, it is always worthwhile to be realistic about your abilities. If you tackle something that is incredibly complex at the beginning of your new watercolour hobby, it may well put you off painting before you have completed the piece. Accept your current level and although you should try to improve it with each painting you begin, remember that this will happen slowly over time. Enjoy painting and eventually you will improve enough to tackle difficult subjects.

Paint something abstract

Sometimes, you need to forget about painting something specific and instead unleash your creativity. Put on some music to inspire you and start to paint something abstract. While abstract painting isn't everyone's choice, it's a great way to get excited about colour.

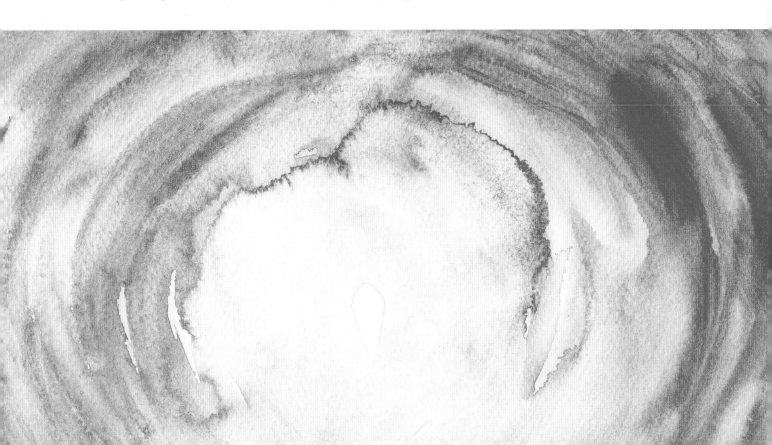

Colour wheel

Artists have combined the spectrum of colour with the emotional reaction to colours to create the colour wheel. The colours of the colour wheel can be divided into primary, secondary and tertiary colours.

Primary colours

Red, blue and yellow make up the primary colours. These three colours are pure and cannot be created by mixing other colours on the wheel. By mixing these colours, we can create secondary colours.

Secondary colours

If red and yellow are mixed together, orange is created. Violet is created by combining red and blue, and similarly blue and yellow produce green when they are mixed. Orange, violet and green are known as secondary colours.

Tertiary colours

When a primary colour is mixed with the secondary colour closest to it, you will create a tertiary colour. So, yellow and orange combine to create a yellow-orange. Red and orange mixed together produce red-orange. Red and violet create red-violet, blue and violet give blue-violet, blue and green create blue-green, and yellow and green create yellow-green.

Hues, tints, shades and tones

The 12 basic colours or hues can be mixed to create an endless variety of tints, tones and shades. Tints are simply these 12 colours mixed with white to create a pastel shade of the original colour. In much the same way, a darker shade of the colour can be achieved by adding black. However, adding black can quickly destroy your main colour. To tone down a colour, you 'grey it down' by adding black and white.

Mixing colours

*Once you have chosen your palette of colours, you can
begin to mix them to create wonderful colours. In addition
to mixing colours in a mixing well, there are other techniques
you can use to mix colour. These include glazing and
scumbling, both of which are discussed later in the book.*

Mixing wells

To mix colours, you will need your
paints, brushes, some clean water
and a mixing well. It is important the
mixing well doesn't have any paint
residue on it. If the well is dirty, as
soon as you add water to the 'old'
paint, it will be usable again and will
also mix with your new colours.

Mixing the
colour

Taking a clean brush, touch the
bottom of your clean water container
so that the bristles of your brush
open up. Lift your brush out of the
water and slide it against the rim of
your mixing well to create a puddle
of water. How much water you use
will depend of the depth of hue you
are aiming for. Now, stroke your
brush against the top of the pigment
to pick up the colour. When you have
sufficient colour, mix this with the
little puddle of water. It is a good idea
to test your colour before you add it
to your painting.

Adding a second colour

In you are mixing two colours together, without rinsing your brush, pick up colour, add it to the little puddle of colour and mix it in. Don't worry about contaminating your paints. Once they have dried, wet them a little and use a clean piece of kitchen towel to wipe over the top of the paint. While you can mix several different colours together, if you mix too many, you will create a muddy puddle of brown. It is best to mix just two colours and never more than three.

How much to mix?

There is nothing more frustrating than running out of a mixed colour before you have finished painting. To help prevent this, it is a good idea to mix more paint than you think you will need. It doesn't matter if you have paint left over – you can always wet it next time you use it to make it usable.

Wet into wet

'Wet into wet', 'wet on wet' or 'wet in wet'
are three names used for the same technique.
As its names suggest, this is painting onto a wet
surface so that the paint flows over the paper.

Using wet into wet

The results of wet into wet are unpredictable and as a result, this technique can frustrate those painters who like to control their work. It also requires a fast way of working, because the work has to be finished before the first layers have dried. You need to work quickly and decisively if you choose to paint on wet paper. If you use only wet into wet to complete your painting, you will create atmosphere and a softer, diffused look. It is especially useful in painting weather, capturing movement and diffusing shapes.

Choosing your paper

Choosing the right type of paper is essential for wet into wet painting. A heavier paper is preferred because it will not crinkle as moisture is added, unlike lighter-weight paper. While hot-pressed paper will allow colours to float over the surface of the paper, cold-pressed and rougher paper will absorb more colour. To find the best paper for your needs, take a small sample of different papers and try a test patch to see which paper gives the desired effect.

24

How to do it

To paint wet into wet, you need to have access to clean water. Because of this, wet into wet is not best suited to watercolour painting outdoors.

Step 1: Wet your paper with a damp sponge or wide brush and clean water. Your paper should be completely saturated. You also need to wet the paper evenly, otherwise your wash will be uneven, too.

Step 2: Mix your colours and apply a flat wash of a single colour. Use the largest brush available for this first wash so that you can work as quickly as possible.

Step 3: While the surface is still wet, add a second and third colour. If you feel that you want more blending, tilt and move your paper to control the flow of colour on the surface. Conversely, if you feel they are 'out of control' simply mop them with some kitchen paper.

Wet on dry

*Watercolourists don't always use a wet into wet technique.
In some instances, they use a 'wet on dry' technique, in which
the wet paint is applied to a dry surface. The dry surface can be
a clean sheet of paper or one that has an already-dry wash on it.*

When to use wet on dry

The wet on dry painting technique is used to create precise lines and a
clear line with strong contrasts. If the area you need to paint is small or
quite distinct, you would be better using a wet on dry method. To apply
paint using wet on dry, apply your wash and then wait for the paper to be
completely dry before applying more paint. You will need to wait for each
colour to dry before you use another.

Transparency

Wet on dry works because watercolours are transparent. However, depending
on how much water you use, the paints will be more or less transparent.
The best way to test how certain layers work, is to use a spare piece of paper
to practise. Do remember though, different papers affect the transparency
of the paint. With this in mind, it may be a good idea to test your paint on
various kinds of paper before you begin. This way, you can see which paper
will best suit your subject.

Glazing

Glazing is a wet on dry technique that is most often associated with oil and acrylic painting. However, it can also be successfully used in watercolour painting to lay thin, transparent washes of colour over each other. For a glaze to be successfully applied, the paper must be completely dry, otherwise the colour will diffuse and create a muddy effect. Because watercolours are transparent, they let light pass through them so the underlying colours of the glaze will shine through and give your work a lovely glow.

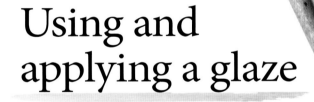

Using and applying a glaze

Glazing can be used to darken or change an individual colour. By applying a glaze to an entire painting, you can create a softer, more atmospheric feel. Because you are painting one colour over another, you need to use paints that are transparent so that the colour can shine through. To apply a glaze, use a soft brush to apply the palest colour first and let it dry completely, then add the next layer. This layer should be just a little darker than the previous one. Don't apply too many layers – two or three should suffice.

Patience is a virtue

It takes a great deal of patience to paint using wet on dry because each layer of paint must be completely dry before you can add the next one. One way to dry a painting is to use a hair dryer. This may sound like a simple task but it can be tricky because you need to dry the paper evenly. If the paper dries unevenly, it may buckle. Don't turn the hair dryer up high, even if you are desperate to continue working on your painting. By using a high setting, you could turn the water into steam or you could even scorch your paper. Keep the dryer on a low setting and hold it a good distance away from your painting – about 25 centimetres (10 inches). If you're working on unstretched paper, use the hair dryer on the back of the sheet as well as the front. If you really cannot wait for a layer to dry, rather than mess up your painting, start a second painting and take it in turns to work on each one.

Is it dry?

Because your paper needs to be completely dry before you can paint the next layer, you'll need to test it to see if it is dry. If you touch the painting, oils from your fingers could transfer onto the paper, which might ruin your work. One way to tell is to hover your hand just above the painting. If the painting feels cool, it is probably still damp.

Adding a tint

You don't need to limit your painting
to paint and brushwork alone. By using
the wet on dry technique, you can add a
coloured tint to a pen or pencil drawing.
This will give the drawing a lovely, soft
glow. To be able to do this, you'll need
to draw your subject in a lot of detail.
You'll need to go beyond drawing just
the basic shapes and add tonal values to
give your drawing the illusion of depth.
Once you are happy with your drawing,
you can paint a flat wash over the pencil.
Choose a colour that will accentuate the
drawing and complement the shading.
In this example the artist has done the
drawing with a colour pencil as well as a
soft graphite pencil. The colour wash is a
lighter shade of the colour pencil.

Combining wet and dry

Most watercolourists will use a combination of wet and dry techniques – it is almost impossible not to. Both techniques add something to a painting. Wet into wet provides a fusion of tones and the wet on dry creates precision.

When to combine

Using wet into wet you can create a softer, blurry background to a painting. For example, when painting flowers or still lifes, you can use wet into wet for the background but a wet on dry technique to capture the detail in the subjects. You can also use a combination of techniques to create perspective. Use wet on dry to capture the detail in the foreground of your painting but use wet into wet to paint the background. The blurriness and lack of detail in the background will give the illusion of distance.

30

Plan your painting

One of the biggest issues when combining painting techniques is to know how long each layer of paint will take to dry. Painting on a wet surface will provide a very different look and feel from that created by painting on a dry surface. To overcome this problem, plan your painting well so that you know which layers to apply first and how long they will take to dry. Think very carefully about the different layers you want to use and which technique will need to be used for which layer. Once you have a clear idea in your head, write it down if need be, or do a rough sketch with annotations.

Adding paint to paper

With your plan at the forefront of your mind, you can start to apply your paint. To use the wet into wet technique on just a small portion of a painting, apply the water to the portion of the paper where you want the final wet into wet watercolour paint. Amazingly, the paint will stay in the boundaries of the water, as long as you do not use too much force when you apply the paint. Because adding water to a painting can become messy, it is more logical to paint all the wet-into-wet layers of your painting first. Once these layers are completely dry, then you can start with the wet in dry work.

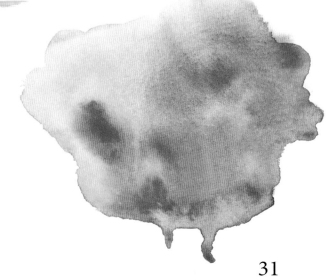

31

Dry brush

Dry brush is another watercolour technique used in combination with other techniques. In this technique, an opaque colour is put over a darker colour in broken patches by rolling the brush. The darker colour shows through the lighter one.

Creating textures

The dry brush technique is very effective in creating texture with watercolours, something that can be difficult to achieve. It can be used to give the look and 'feel' of rough tree bark, froth on a wave or a gritty road surface. It can also be used to create the texture of hair in portraiture.

Adding focus

Dry brush produces very crisp, hard-edged marks. Because these marks are so distinct, they can really enhance a focal point if they are used around it. However, if used incorrectly, they may detract from your intended focal point. For example, if you use dry brush in the background of a landscape painting, the focus will shift to the background of your painting, creating a feeling of imbalance.

The final result

There are a number of factors that will affect the final result of your dry brush strokes. These are:

• Part of brush used: if you are painting with a round brush, you can use the side of the brush and allow the point to touch the paper. You can also just use the bulb part of the brush without the point touching the paper. Each of these will create a different effect.

• Paper type: dry brush can be used on any watercolour paper type but it is much easier to create using a dry brush stroke on rough, textured paper.

• Speed of brush movement: the speed of your movement will need to be determined by the paper you are using. If you are using smooth paper you need to move the brush very fast to create this type of stroke.

• Dryness of paper: this kind of stroke can be produced only on dry or slightly damp paper. It is more difficult to create the right effect on damp paper.

• Paint: the amount of paint on your brush and its consistency is important. The wetter your brush, the faster you will need to work.

Blending

Blending, or charging, as it is sometimes called, is a watercolour technique where colour is mixed on paper rather than in a mixing well or palette. Blending allows a smooth transition between colours, and can also create the illusion of shadow.

How to blend two colours

Tilt your paper and then fully load your brush with the first colour. Establish your watercolour bead and paint the top of the area you wish to paint. Rinse out your brush and blot it well. Now, fully load your watercolour brush with the second colour. Lightly touch the bead with the tip of your brush and continue to release more colour. Make a light, bouncing motion with your brush as you work your way across to the other side of the bead. Your new watercolour bead will now be a blend of the two colours. Paint with this new watercolour bead until it decreases in size. Rinse out your brush and then load it with the second colour again. Charge it into the mixed colour bead and finish painting the area.

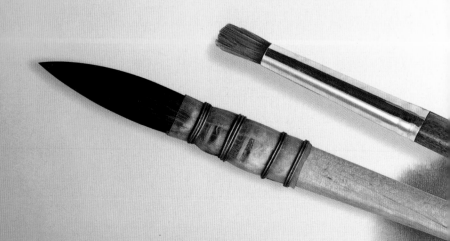

34

Reverse the colours

Once you are comfortable blending the colours, you can try reversing them midway. So your paper will start with the first colour, which will be blended into the second colour. This will then be blended again with the first colour. This takes a bit of practice, but the end result will be worth it.

Charging small details

You can use charging on areas as small as a flower petal. To do this, load your brush with the first colour, then blot it lightly on a tissue. Paint as far as you would like your first watercolour to go, touching your brush lightly to the paper with each stroke. Rinse your brush and blot it very well before loading your brush with the second colour. Blot your brush lightly on the tissue. With overlapping, light brush strokes, charge the two watercolours together. Rinse your brush and blot well. You'll need to work quickly because the charge won't work if the paint dries.

Brushwork

Watercolour painting is unforgiving and it is not always possible to correct or amend bad brushwork, so you need to think carefully about your brushwork before you begin to paint.

The right brush

There are several factors that influence brushwork:

• Types of brush: as you know, brushes come in a multitude of different shapes, sizes and bristle type. Each of these brushes can produce a wealth of strokes. While many artists favour a couple of brushes, it is a good idea to experiment and practise with all the brushes in your box. Try to observe the many different strokes you can create with each brush.

• Area of brush: the surface area of your brush that you use can create different strokes – for example, using more of your brush will create a different stroke from the one you'll produce if you use a smaller area of it.

• Pressure applied: how much pressure you apply to the brush when making your strokes will also affect your brushwork. The more pressure applied, the fatter the line.

• Wetness of your brush: the wetness of your brush will completely change not just the colour of your strokes, but also the lines they create.

• Speed of marks: the faster you work, the less time your paint has to dry.

Choosing a subject

Landscapes

Scenes of nature that feature mountains, forests, gardens, lakes and other water scenes are called landscapes. Today, landscapes are very popular and most artists will have attempted a landscape scene at some point. However, landscapes haven't always been highly valued. In the past, painting of natural scenes was considered lower in status than other subject matter, such as portraiture.

Choosing a subject

The first step to painting a landscape scene is to find something to paint! To do this, you'll need to choose a viewpoint. Where you stand will determine what you see and the angle at which you see it. Take your time – you should spend as much time observing the landscape as you do drawing it.

To help find the best view, you can use a viewfinder. Try to find something that has interesting colour combinations or stands out, for example a blue sky against a tree with autumnal leaves. While you might be tempted to put everything you see on your paper, you don't have to. Rather, choose the strongest elements, those that give the landscape its characteristic look, and paint them.

While you can control the light of a still life painting, controlling natural light can be difficult. The light will change depending on the time of day and the season. To combat these changes, you will need to view your scene at the same time each day. This isn't entirely convenient because you'll also have to paint quickly to avoid the light changing as time passes. Instead, you can take a photograph of the scene. Make a copy of the photograph and annotate it with notes about the light.

Getting the composition right

There is no rule that says you have to paint the landscape exactly as you see it. You can rearrange the elements to suit your composition. It usually works best if your painting has more detail in the foreground and less detail in the background. However, you will need to play around with different compositions to find what works best for you. To work out the best composition, do several different thumbnail sketches. If you feel that there are several compositions that 'work', you can paint them all, creating a series of landscapes. If you are doing just one painting, your thumbnails should help you to decide where to draw your horizon line.

Portraits

You only need to visit a portrait gallery to see that people have been 'sitting' for portraits for centuries. In years gone by, paying someone to paint your likeness was a sign of wealth and power. While professionals did these paintings, for the beginner watercolourist, portrait painting can be daunting and difficult.

Painting a likeness

As an artist, it is your job to capture a likeness of a person and this means capturing more than just their outer appearance: you need to capture his or her inner person, too. This sounds scary in itself, but if you want to be a successful portrait painter, you need to see the person you're painting, the sitter, as any other three dimensional subject.

Proportion

The first step in capturing this likeness is to understand the proportions that make up a face and to sketch the basic shapes of the face. By following these simple rules, your portrait will be in proportion and your painting will have a balanced feel:

• A person's eyes are always half way up his or her head.

• The eyebrow is above the half-way point of the head on a person with a normal, not receding, hairline. On young children, the head is larger and the child's features are lower down.

• The distance from the hairline to the eyebrow, the eyebrow to the underside of the nose, and from the underside of the nose to the chin are almost exactly the same. This splits the face into thirds.

• The tops of ears are usually in line with the eyebrow and the lobe with the bottom of the nose. However, as people age, their ears grow larger and their lobes hang lower.

• If your sitter is looking straight, the corners of his or her mouth line up with the pupils.

• There is exactly room for a third eye between the eyes.

• The underside of the bottom lip usually falls halfway between the underside of the nose and the chin.

What happens if you want to paint a three-quarter profile? In this case, these proportions will still work, but you will see a quarter of the width of the mouth. The corner of the furthest eye from you will now be hidden by the bridge of the nose, but its centre should still line up with the corner of the mouth. The angle will also mean that the iris will become more elliptical.

Animals

There are so many different animals to paint, from furry pets and wild animals such as giraffes and bears, to birds with striking feathers and fish with scales. Each animal will present a different challenge, but the basic principles are much the same.

Background

If you want your animal to be the main focus of your painting, choose your background accordingly. For example, fish in a pool of water or a cat curled up on the sofa will be the main focus, so the background should not detract from the animal. Your animal may be part of a larger painting, too. You could paint a waterscape and include the fish, or paint a landscape and have a giraffe near to one of the trees. In these cases, the animals need to attract the viewer's eye so should be the focal point of the painting.

Make a study

It's always better to paint a live subject. That way, you get to know the subject and understand the animal. The more time you spend with an animal the easier it will be to paint. Obviously, painting live isn't always possible: you may not have access to the animal and most often, the animal will not sit still and wait for you to finish your labour of love!

To make your study of the animal, you will need to use a combination of drawing it live and taking photographs. Take as many photographs as possible from different angles. Before you start drawing, choose the best photograph that you feel captures the animal's character and use that as your reference. However, you will still benefit from drawing some of the features live. For example, eyes and feet are hard to see in a photograph. The muscles and movement of the animal may also be difficult to capture on camera, especially if the animal is black in colour, so you may need to do some quick sketches of these.

Seeing the colours

A black animal is rarely black and a white animal rarely white. There are many colours that make up the black or white of an animal. To make sure you get these right, spend time observing the animal and noting the colours that you actually see. This will prove invaluable when it comes to mixing your paints. You'll be able to mix your own black paint, rather than use black from a tube or pan, capturing the subtle shades in it.

Drawing

One of the most important steps in painting your animal is to draw it first. Drawing the animal helps to get the proportions right and it also gives you a chance to check that you are happy with the composition of your painting. If you are drawing from a photograph, use a pair of dividers to get the proportions more precise. Work out what the ratio of your photograph to paper is. Measure the part of the animal you are drawing with the dividers and use the ratio to multiply it to give you the measurement for your drawing. To draw the animal, look for the basic shapes. Every subject can be broken down in to basic geometric shapes. Draw these basic shapes and then add the lines to complete the outline of your animal.

Still life

A still life is a depiction of inanimate objects, such as fruit, vegetables, bottles, vases and musical instruments. For centuries, artists have been painting still lifes and for most people starting to paint with watercolours, still lifes offer the perfect opportunity to combine different techniques and skills.

Composition

Still life subjects are more simple than most because they don't move. How you arrange them is how you will paint them. However, getting the composition of these objects right is not always as straightforward as it seems. The arrangement of objects needs to create visual harmony. If you place the objects too close together, they become heavy on the eye. If they are too far apart, the composition won't work either. To check if the composition is working, set up the subject, step back to where you will be sitting when you paint and look carefully. If it isn't working, make the necessary alterations and then go back to where you will be sitting and have another look.

Focal point

You will need to have a focal point for your composition to work. One way to work this out is to close your eyes, open them and look at your set up and shut them again as rapidly as possible. What you see in that glimpse is your focal point. This is what you will need to emphasise in your painting.

46

Working from photographs

It is always better to leave your still life set up until you are finished painting it. However, this may not always be possible – you may need to use some of the objects or you may have to share your workspace with other people. If this is the case, take a photograph of the still life. Try to take it with as much natural light on it as possible. You can then photocopy the photograph and either trace it onto your paper or draw it with a grid.

Light

Light is very important in all paintings, but it is of particular importance to still life painting because the inanimate objects can be brought to life by the light that shines on them. It is preferential to set up your still life scene near a natural light source. The part of an object closest to the light source is usually the brightest and lightest. These bright areas are called the highlights. Highlights can be created by leaving the white of the paper to show through or by using masking fluid. The objects further from the light source are the medium and then the darkest tones. Shadows are darkest next to the object and lighter as you move away from the object.